Alice Parker

FOLKSONG TRANSFORMATIONS

Singing and Responding to Folksongs:

A Primer for Improvisation

Hinshaw Music

"The Chickens They Are Crowing" is from the collection *English Folksongs from the Southern Appalachians* collected by Cecil J. Sharp and edited by Maud Karpeles. It is used with the kind permission of Oxford University Press.

ISBN: 0-937276-25-1

CONTENTS

Introduction to the Second Edition

A true folk song is one which has been adopted by generations of people as their own, and which exists in several variants. It might possibly have been a composed piece at first, but very few compositions achieve this cross-over into anonymity. Those tunes we know from all over the world survive because they are just right: they have a perfect balance between words, rhythms and pitches, form and function. Most of the time we can't date these tunes, but we do know their geographic origin because of the language of the text, and often we can be sure of, or sense, their function in every-day life (lullaby, work song, love song, lament, etc.). This particular collection was compiled for the class in *Writing for Voices* that I have taught for more than twenty-five years. Because I wanted very specific kinds of melodies for my teaching, it seemed best to make my own compilation of what I call 'pure gold' melodies. Sung with some kind of understanding, these are tunes which 'work' for solos, choirs, group singing, improvising and arranging.

Interpreting

Each single-line melody is a universe of its own -- a scenario -- which comes to life when the singer becomes the song. For the song is not what is printed on the page: it is the communication of mood and character by means of words and music. What can be notated is the merest glimpse of this universe. It comes alive through human intervention, the transformation into meaningful sound.

Look on these melodies, then, as exercises in the re-creation of song, rather than a sight-reading manual. Notation of folk-melodies is different from notation of a composed song: what is printed is only one suggested version of a tune which exists in many variants. The page here is rather like the skeleton of the song: it gives the performer a framework within which to work, without specifying the details. To unlock the song, begin with the words: implicit in the poetry are tempo, color, mood, characterization, function, form, dynamics, climax and even specific durations. Think about these approaches, decide which verses you want to use in which order, then read the text aloud in rhythm, being careful not to lose the subtleties of speech when following the notation. Finally, let the curve of pitches transform the poem into song.

The great challenge is to sing or play the song in such a way that it is totally convincing both to performer and to listener. Except for one example in each chapter no interpretive markings are given, for each performer must recreate, in his or her own terms, this endlessly variable microcosmos. There is no accompaniment, since the channel of communication is to be the individual human voice. Additional verses are given not only for the 'story,' but to allow practise in the art of variation: how does one verse differ from another? (Singers training for solo careers should begin with this approach: it illumines the whole process of studying composed songs.)

Pitch and Rhythm

Any song is a combination of pitches, rhythms and words. It seems reasonable to me that about half the songs in the world might count rhythm as their most important feature, and the other half discount 'beat' in favor of rhythmic freedom and the accompanying emphasis on melodic curve with time to savor the text. Gregorian Chant is a pure example of the latter, and any toe-tapping tune for dancing is unmistakably the former. So the first question you might ask any melody is: Are you a pitch piece, or a rhythm piece?

I've learned in teaching, arranging, and in leading SINGS, to begin with a pitch piece: it gets people out of their familiar patterns, they learn that they must listen to each other to stay together, and they must focus on the most melodic parts of their own voices and the text being sung. This kind of freedom is difficult to comprehend at first, when the familiar songs are all written in clear meters. But awareness of the possibility of this freedom, the mood which it establishes, and the beauties of the subtle interplay of accent and duration in the text, combine to create, time after time, a very moving musical experience.

In pitch pieces, tones and words govern the rhythm: high notes or important syllables can be lengthened, there is time to breathe at the end of each phrase, and there is no compulsion to hurry. In dances, on the other hand, nothing is allowed to disturb the beat -- and this defines the way the words are sung and the way we breathe. The main thing is to keep going.

Responding
The "scenario" idea includes not only a singer, but a listener -- one who responds. For practising this form of improvisation, try singing with a partner: one on melody in a way that creates a sound-world, the other listening and responding to this particular sound-world, filling in the breath-pauses, reflecting back not only memorable turns of phrase but also the mood and color of the original. This is the beginning of counterpoint, which is melody's response to melody. The first attempts should be vocal, complete with words; later, if you are an instrumentalist, try answering within the characteristic sound of your own instrument.

Notating
We've been talking about finding the sound of a melody. Writing it down is another matter of great concern to the writer and reader. The system we use is excellent for rhythmic pieces; it is positively unhelpful in suggesting freedom from pulse. In fact, freedom is un-notable: we can't even notate exactly a simple English phrase like "Hello, how are you?" So we must learn to bend the notation to the needs of the song, recognizing that we read rhythmic pieces totally differently from 'free' ones. The questions should be: How closely can we notate the melody to show how we sing it -- here, now? How many marking are necessary, or helpful? How do we choose a key and a meter? Can we change notes and/or words from our source? How specific do we need to be? In folk music, all these are open questions: there is no original text to refer back to as the authority.

The Sequencing of this Book
The form of this book is dictated by the sequence of my teaching: **chant** (to learn listening, freedom in rhythm, and freedom from the tyranny of the page); **pentatonic songs** (for sensing scale plus beat and easy answers); **modal melodies** (for counterpoint); then **tonal songs** (for dealing with traditional harmonies). The final chapter is dedicated to **blues and jazz** which encompass all the preceding varieties of song, and are the easiest melodies of all for group improvisation.

One song is chosen for rather lengthy analysis at the beginning of each chapter. Comments are made about the *text* as a separate poem, the *melody* as a musical unity of pitches, rhythms and form; the *context* out of which one performance of the tune can grow (there are as many as the human imagination can devise); one possible *interpretation* (which notates the preceding context); *ornamentation and variation* of the single-line melody; and finally some comments about a possible *response* from one sympathetic and willing listener. This encapsulates my teaching of choral arranging, which begins with a characteristic performance of the melody and ends with a two-part a cappella arrangement which carries within itself the possibility of further extensions in voicing and accompaniment. The video *Folksong Transformations* illustrates the teaching of melodic improvisation.

So, enjoy and use this collection in many ways. Teach yourself to be a wonderful folk-singer, by learning to imagine and perform these songs in a way that compels others to listen and join in. Analyze the melodies to discover the incredibly complex combination of checks and balances which make up tunes that last. Play with vocal and instrumental answers to discover what the melody is implying. And then write your own arrangement, for your own group. Bask in the riches of these tunes, and collect others which offer commensurate rewards in the singing, listening and joining in.

ALICE PARKER

I. CHANT STYLE MELODIES

In singing based on text rhythms, the articulation of the single-line melody is crucial. (Let us define articulation as the way any and every single note, phrase and verse is begun, continued and released, including all the interpretive possibilities of color, dynamics, tempo and diction, as well as pitch and rhythmic play.) First practice reading aloud, listening to inflections, pauses, punctuation; and to shades of meaning and how the voice conveys them. Imagine that you are an actor in a very resonant space, and must speak more slowly and clearly than usual to reach the listener.

Now try intoning one phrase of the song—words chanted on one pitch. Can you keep all the subtleties of the speaking? Don't let it get 'measured' in any way: the rule is that each syllable is different in length, accent and intensity from those on either side. Then add the pitches of the melody to the same phrase. Is it still 'free'? wonderfully expressive? unhurried? intensely communicative?

In all these melodies, the success of the response is totally dependent on the singing just heard: the response should unerringly echo the mood, accents and durations of the model. In chant singing, the principal function of a response is to support, while keeping out of the way: it should not do anything that will restrict the freedom of the solo melody. Cadential echoes, pedals and antiphony are all the devices needed.

Oh, Shenandoah

Appalachian

2. Oh, Shenandoah, I love your daughter,
Way hay, you rolling river.
Oh, Shenandoah, I love your daughter,
Way hay, we're bound away,
'Cross the wide Missouri.

3. Oh, Shenandoah, I'm bound to leave you,
Way hay, you rolling river.
Oh, Shenandoah, I'll not deceive you,
Way hay, we're bound away,
'Cross the wide Missouri.

Text: There are many variants of this song, which is often listed as a sea-chanty. Some chanties are work songs, with the rhythmic drive needed to accompany heavy labor; but this is a 'fo' castle' song, sung in the living quarters of the ship in the evening when work is done. Often about memories of home and past loves, these chanties recycle familiar verses and ideas in texts with much repetition. Note the intricate shape of each verse: an expository line, a response, another story line (or repeat of the first), then a different response, all culminating in a 5th line of still another response. These particular verses tell a fragmentary love story: 'Shenandoah' can refer to an Indian chief, or a river or county in Virginia. The indecision is part of the spell.

Tune: This is a 'rangy' melody with a span of an eleventh in the first two phrases: It is intended to be sung by real voices, with a rich sound. The meter here alternates between 4/4 and 3/4, indicating freedom from a fixed rhythm. It would be possible to sing it in a steady duple meter, but I much prefer it in a more improvised manner, where even the vestige of steady pulse disappears. I often challenge my students to come up with a more pictorial notation: this example combines some of their ideas.

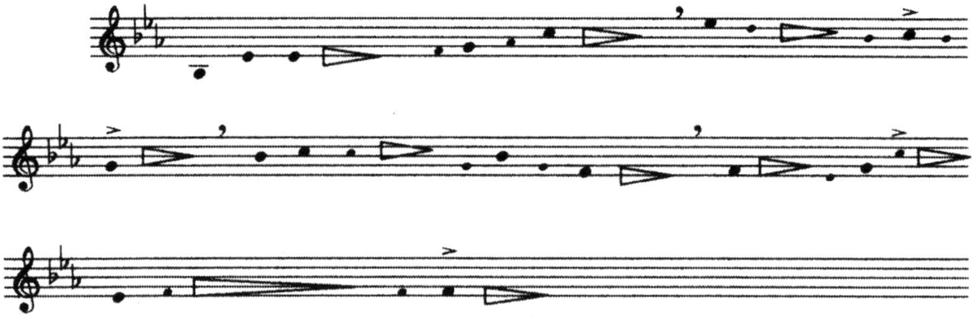

Notice that this concept of freedom does not keep you from 'snapping' the beat at "river" and "away". You are exploring the boundary between measured and unmeasured rhythm, finding how much you can open up the beat. How long can you hold *this* loaded syllable? How can *those* long notes be varied within their span by changes in dynamics and tone-color? How can the text be colored by cherishing both vowels and consonants as expressive-devices? How much silence can there be between phrases or verses?

Context: If I am remembering something or someone from long ago, the distance from the place and emotion gives a plaintive color to the voice. I'm in no hurry to get through the song: the memories flooding up fill the spaces between notes and phrases. I can color my voice differently for the 'story' lines of the text, and what might have been group responses. . .

One possible interpretation:

Note: is this over-marked? I think so, because there are seemingly contradictory instructions, which impede clarity. I want to trust that a singer will always diminuendo into an unaccented syllable, and will always feel the climax points of a tune. I much prefer the empty, or almost-empty page.

Ornamentation and Variation:

Think the form through all three verses: how does one differ from another? Can this difference be notated? Can you supply an adjective or adverb for each verse to denote the difference? Is there a sense of progression through all three? Are the fermatas the same length in each verse, or are they truly free? Or can you decide which needs to be the longest one?

Responses:

This song works wonderfully in two parts antiphonally, with the held notes at the ends of phrases becoming pedal tones under the answers. Solo-response is also possible: how do you handle the 5th line in each verse? Or, it can be sung by one voice throughout, with the other echoing bits of phrase during the fermatas. With a large group, suggest that the melody by sung by one solo voice, while the others listen and respond very softly, echoing different parts of the melody at different times and speeds. The effect is that of an echo chamber, where the melody stirs to life different pitches and curves, surrounding itself with its own vibrations. It can be truly magical.

Black, Black, Black

Appalachian
(from the British Isles)

2. Oh, I love my love, and well she knows,
I love the ground whereon she goes.
If you no more on earth I see,
I can't serve you as you have me.

3. Winter's past, and the leaves now again are green:
The time has past that we have seen,
But still I hope the time will come
When you and I will be as one.

By'm Bye

Appalachian Lullaby

2. By'm bye, by'm bye,
Stars shining,
Number, number four, number five, number six,
Good Lord, etc.

3. By'm bye, by'm bye,
Stars shining,
Number, number sev'n, number eight, number nine, *
Good Lord, etc.

* (I always add "number ten".)
—*Alice Parker*

He's Gone Away

Appalachian

FORM: Refrain, Verse 1, Refrain, Verse 2, Refrain, Coda.

II. PENTATONIC MELODIES

There are only five tones in this scale ('penta' is the Greek word for 'five') which is in use over most of the globe. The black notes on the piano give you this 'gapped' scale, where there are no half-steps and two one-and-a-half step intervals.

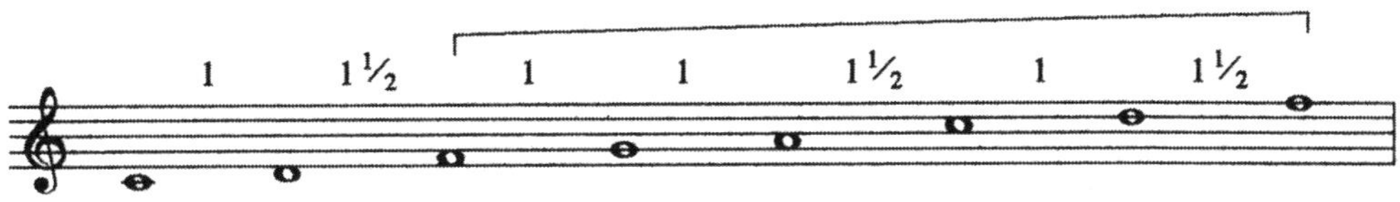

Since harmonic motion is not implied in the scale, most of these melodies will sound 'right' over a pedal or drone. Echoes and answers using the same tones will always fit: pentatonic songs are made for improvising.

Now pulse and meter are added to the pure melody of the first chapter. No longer can we play with words with freedom: we are harnessed to the beat, and have to squeeze the syllables in and catch a breath where it's possible. After you define the dance (and actually dance it if you can), learn to keep it going relentlessly. Variation comes mainly in the number of measures between verses -- or between phrases -- or, the number of pulses in a measure (if it is a fun piece, and you want some metric play.) Find one tempo and quality of beat and stick to it. For responses, ostinato patterns may be based on a just-heard text phrase, or a refrain; a witty duet-duel can be improvised on the spot by an accomplished text-contrapuntalist (like a rap-singer!)

Frog Went A-Courtin'

2. [He] rode down to Miss Mousie's door, . . .
Where he'd often been before . . .

3. Little Miss Mousie came tripping down, . . .
In her silk and satin gown. . .

4. He took Miss Mousie on his knee . . .
Said, "Miss Mousie, will you marry me?" . .

5. "Without my uncle Rat's consent . . .
I would not marry the Pres-i-dent.". .

6. Uncle Rat gave his consent, . . .
The weasel wrote the publishment. . .

7. The old Rat laughed till he shook his fat sides . . .
To think Miss Mousie would be a bride.

Text: This song is found in many collections, in many forms. Here, only the pre-nuptial verses are used: there's not room for the 24 in my source! Other versions list the different animals arriving, and describe obviously a play song, meant to amuse a child, or for a group to dance or act out.

Tune: At first hearing, this simple melody sounds like an 'easy' song in a major key. But it has wonderful complexities built in, the first being that absence of the 4th and 7th tones of the familiar major scale, and the second its phrase structure with an a-symmetrical, three-part form. Other variants have three statements of the first line, which give you a traditional four-phrase structure; I much prefer this (although you have a right to argue for the variant which you know best!) Look at the form: first phrase, 4 bars (2+2); second, 2 bars repeating line 1 of the poem; and third, 4 bars (2+2); with new text, and the music repeating the 2nd half of the first phrase. It almost demands an extra two bars between verses, to complete a 4 + 4 + 4 structure (echo the Mm-hm?) The high point of the melody is reached in the middle of the song, and similar cadences into "Mm-hm" make it easy to learn and remember. The tempo should be as fast as you can sing the words.

Context: Who are you as you sing this song: a parent? grandparent? older brother or sister? teacher? To whom are you singing? What is their response? Could you keep a whole roomful of kindergartners in motion with your singing? Imagine what instruments you would like to have playing along (banjo? jug-bass?), and hear them in your head as you sing -- you'll sing better.

(Note how little chance there is for the kind of text play we found in chapter one... we just have to keep moving too fast. Here, the difference has to be in the style of singing [English accent or rough folk etc]; and in tempo and beat: where and how much you accent. The little 'x's in the music indicate syllables that might be spoken rather than sung.)

Ornamentation and Variation: No time for it! The different numbers of syllables in different verses give you the possibility of melodic variation, and imitating different animals as you sing changes the vocal color. Also: how many ways can you sing "Mm-hm"? (Don't forget that you might even *speak* one line in rhythm -- just don't over-do it).

Responses: "Mm-hm" in the text is a gift from heaven: use it. Where does it first come? Next? How often? How might it expand into more echoes? (Don't let the echoes interfere with your hearing new text: every time you sing the song, pretend it is the *first* time.) How do the verses connect? Do some belong close together; or do some need 3 or 4 or 5 or 16 (!) bars betweeen? Do you need a coda? How do you stop this energy-generating beat?

hm.
5. "With-
"Miss Mous-ie, Miss Mous-ie, will you mar-ry me, Mm -
out my Un-cle Rat's con-sent, Mm - hm.
With-
hm.
Miss - Mous-ie, Miss Mous-ie, Mm -
out my Un-cle Rat's con - sent, I would not mar-ry the Pres - i-dent!"
hm,
Miss Mous-ie, Mm - hm.
Mm -
Un - cle
hm,
Mm - hm?

Buckeye Jim

American Traditional

2. Way up yonder above the moon,
A blue-jay nests in a silver spoon.
Buckeye Jim . . .

3. Way down yonder in a wooden trough,
Woman's sick of the whoopin' cough.
Buckeye Jim . . .

4. Way down yonder on a hollow log,
A red bird danced with a green bullfrog.
Buckeye Jim . . .

How Can I Keep From Singing?

English Quaker

2. When tyrants tremble, sick with fear,
And hear their death-knells ringing,
When Friends rejoice, both far and near,
How can I keep from singing?
In prison cell and dungeon vile
Our thoughts to them are winging;
When Friends by shame are undefiled:
How can I keep from singing?

The Riddle Song

British Isles

2. How can there be a cherry without a stone?
   How can there be a chicken without a bone?
   How can there be a ring without an end?
   How can there be a baby with no crying?

3. A cherry when it's blooming, it has no stone;
   A chicken when it's pipping, it has no bone;
   A ring when it's rolling, it has no end;
   A baby when it's sleeping, there's no crying.

III. MODAL MELODIES

Mode is simply another word for scale; in European music, modes are the kinds of scales used from about 400 - 1600 C.E. Major and minor scales are both modes, but only came into prominence in the Baroque period. Here is a quick diagram for beginners (consult a music dictionary for more detailed information).

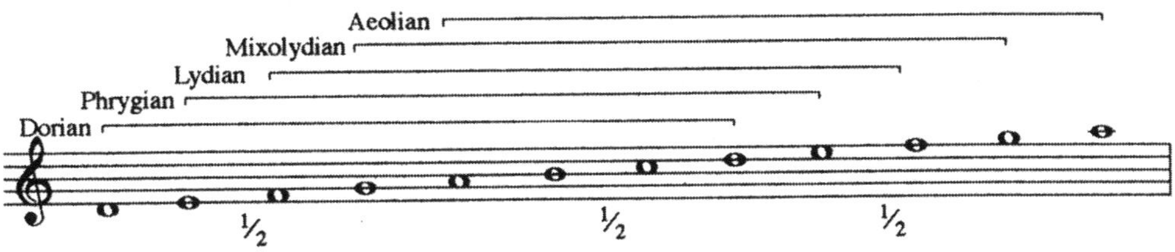

Be aware that the beginning note of each mode, and the final note of each modal tune, is the home tone; accustom your ears to feeling 'at home' at the end. The songs do not end on the 'wrong' note, nor do they carry an emotional content of 'sad'; listening with 20th century ears may expect major to be 'happy', and everything else less so.

Modes do not imply the same kinds of harmony that we are used to in tonal music (see the next chapter). They are much more open to pedals and free imitation. Decide if your melody is a pitch piece or a rhythm piece, and then listen to the curves of the melody, restricting your answers to the notes in the melody itself.

I Am In Love

Southern United States

REFRAIN

O love is warming, love is charming,

And love is handsome while it's new;

But as love grows older, love grows colder,

And fades away like the morning dew.

2. I wish to God I never had seen him,

Or in his cradle he had died;

To think so fair a lady as I am

Should be in love and be denied.

REFRAIN

Description and Performance Suggestions

Text: This is a variant of *Waly, Waly*, a Britsh folksong, with an old formal speech style: "I dare not own it", "the very pain". This refrain is found in many songs - a philosophical view of unrequited love. By contrast, the verse is intensely personal (it's happening now, to me), and even chilling in the second verse - we're not used to such a frank outburst from the woman's point of view. Read aloud these lines, and listen to the preponderance of pitched consonants - l's, m's and n's. Vary your reading to reflect the character and color of the different sections. Try reading in the rhythm of the song without losing the natural flow of the language.

Tune: This is a variant of the *Poor, Wayfaring Stranger* tune, found in the southern USA, which in turn comes from English balladry. The scale is modal and haunting, the movement disjunct, with a characteristic leap up of a fourth and fifth at the beginnings of phrases 1, 3 and 4. The range is a ninth, up to that pivotal and unique C#. Phrases 1 and 4 share a similar curve, number 2 moves up, and number 3 climaxes at the beginning, then curves down. The meter is triple, but the nature of the song allows freedom to hold the high note, and not to hurry from one phrase to another. The vocal color is rich, the movement legato.

Context: In the verse, the singer is venting interior emotions; confusion, sorrow, love and rage at once. The refrain is calming, distancing. Try for a free play in pitch and rhythm on the verses; be a bit more formal on the refrain; but try adding a few "graces" the second time.

Interpretation:

Here is one possible interpretation. This is not set down as an example of "the right way" to sing this song; it's more of an exercise in trying to notate the un-notatable! There is never one right way, in the same sense that there is no one "correct" oak leaf or snowflake; endless, subtle variation is the norm.

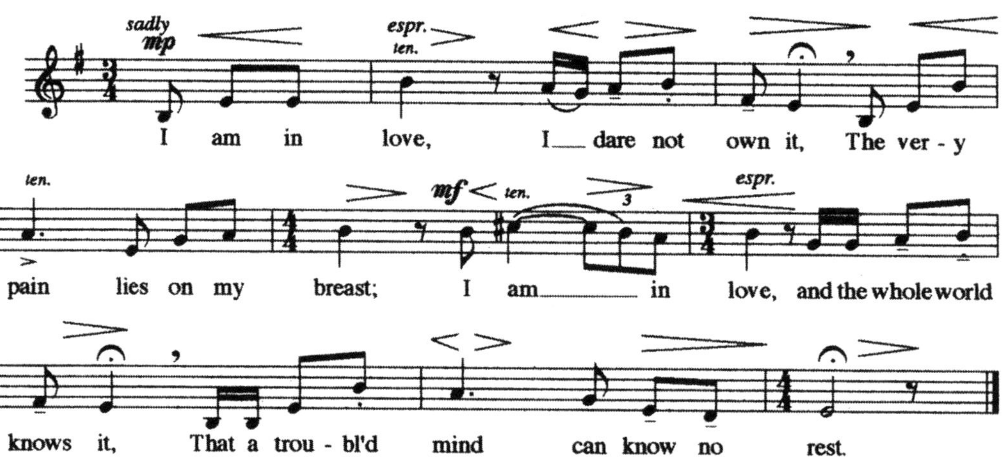

Ornamentation and Variation:

Once the song is begun, it must continue to flow naturally from that beginning. The repetition of the melody in the refrain is seen not as a constraint, but as a release into "endless, subtle variation". And these variations come largely from text-suggestions, from the singer's total commitment to communicating the song. Adding passing notes, changing phrase lengths, coloring words ("warming", "colder", "fades away"), varying the mood at verse 2 - all contribute cues to the singing voice (and to the listening ear).

REFRAIN
mf brighter
O love is warm - ing, love is charm-ing, And love is
hand - some while it's new; But as love grows old - er, love grows
cold - er, And fades a - way like the morn - ing dew.
Verse 2.
mf faster, keep moving
I wish to God I never had seen him, Or in his
cra - dle he had died; To think so fair a la - dy as
I am should be in love and be de - nied.
REFRAIN
p (softer, slower, philosophically)
O love is warm - ing, love is charm - ing, And love is
hand - some while it's new; But as love grows
freely
old-er, love grows cold-er And fades a - way like the morn - ing dew.

Response:

Here is a possible response to this folksong. The long notes in this and similar melodies are "holes" or "windows" which invite filling in: the responder can sing without losing the ongoing line of the solo. The first answer tends to set a pattern which then takes on a life of its own: developing, lengthening, varying, climaxing. The listener is sympathetic, consoling, echoing. There is always time to answer on the second beat (not necessarily every one), with sustained notes on "love", "own it", "pain", etc. This would flower easily into canonic answers in the refrain, where a text ostinato on "O love" seems wholly natural. The responses should never overpower or box-in the melody: let the solo remain free.

I Know Where I'm Going

Irish

2. I have stockings of silk,
And shoes of fine green leather,
Combs to buckle my hair,
And a ring for every finger.

3. Some say he's black,
But I say he's bonny,
Fairest of them all
Is my handsome, winsome Johnny.

4. Feather beds are soft,
And painted rooms are bonny
But I would leave them all,
To go with my love, Johnny.

Soldier, Soldier

Appalachian

2. Off to the hat shop she did go,

For O the fife and drum;

Got him a hat and all fine things,

Now, soldier, put them on.

3. Now, now soldier, won't you marry me?
For O the fife and drum;
How can I marry such a pretty girl as you,
When I've got no coat to put on?

4. So, off to the tailor she did run,
For O the fife and drum;
Got him a coat and all fine things,
Now, soldier, put them on.

5. Soldier, soldier, won't you marry me?
For O the fife and drum;
How can I marry such a pretty girl as you,
When I've got no shoes to put on?

6. Off to the shoe shop she did go,
For O the fife and drum;
Got him a pair of the finest that were there,
Now, soldier, put them on.

7. Now, now, soldier, won't you marry me?
For O the fife and drum;
How can I marry such a pretty girl as you,
With a wife and a baby at home?

The Chickens They Are Crowing

Appalachian

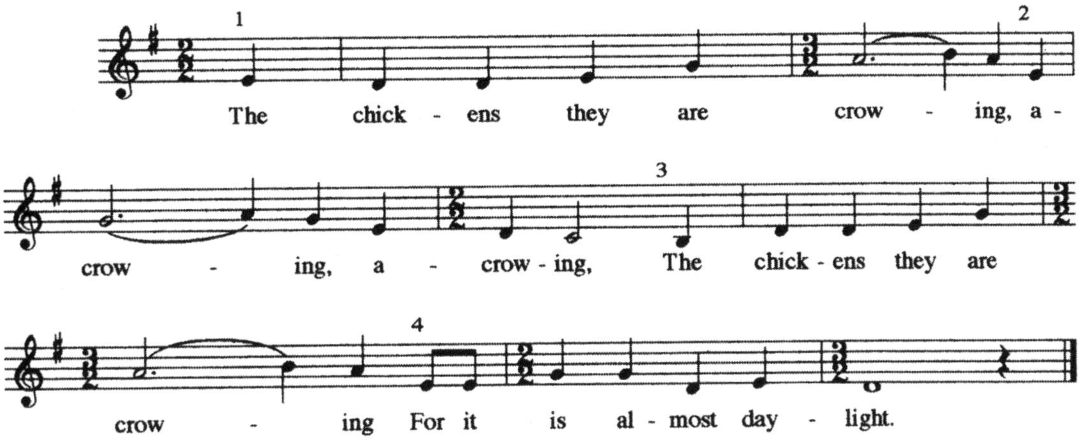

2. My mother she [will scold me, *(3x)*]

My mother she will scold me

For staying away all night.

3. My father he'll [uphold me, *(3x)*]

My father he'll uphold me

And say I've done just right.

4. I won't go home [till morning, *(3x)*]

I won't go home till morning

And I'll stay with the girls all night.

Weevily Wheat

American Square Dance

(no upbeats)

2. Coffee grows on white oak trees,

River flows with brandy;

Choose you one to roam with you,

Sweet as 'lasses candy.
REFRAIN

(no upbeats)

3. Charley's here and Charley's there,

Charley's over the ocean,

Charley, he'll come back some day,

Unless he takes a notion!
REFRAIN

What Shall We Do With The Drunken Sailor?

English Sea Chanty

2. Put him in the long boat until he's sober. *(3x)*
Early in the morning.
REFRAIN

3. Pull out the plug and wet him all over. *(3x)*
Early in the morning.
REFRAIN

4. Tie him to the scuppers with the hose pipe on him. *(3x)*
Early in the morning.
REFRAIN

5. Heave him by the leg in a runnin' bowline. *(3x)*
Early in the morning.
REFRAIN

IV. TONAL MELODIES

Tonal music implies 1) a home tone, 2) a major or minor scale, and 3) triads built of scale tones on each scale step. Here are these components in the key of C major. (Its relative minor is A minor, which has the same key signature, but starts and ends on A, and is often subject to variation in its 6th and 7th steps, which in turn tilts it towards A major.)

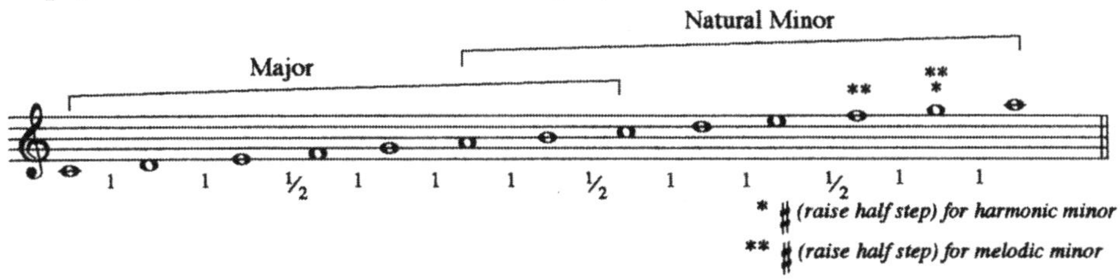

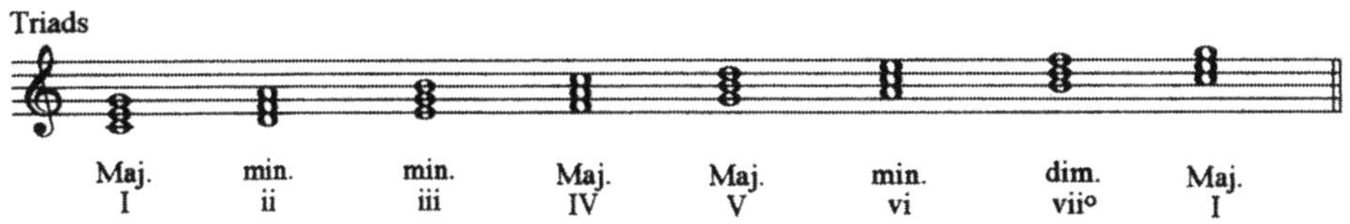

The harmony is an integral part of the melody, and you must be able to identify the chords which the melody implies. (Think of guitar chords, or a simple plucked bass part.) In most folk songs, the harmonic pattern is very simple: I, IV, V, I etc. Don't aproach these songs with the idea of making them more interesting harmonically: accept the simple basic chord pattern, and get variety through playing with text rhythm and pitch ornamentation rather than by "modernizing' the chords. The very simplicity of the harmonic pattern allows an extraordinary melodic and rhythmic variety to be superimposed on it. Use echoes and answers as we did before, but make them fit the harmonic design. It takes a lot more fore-knowledge to do this; it's not so easy to improvise.

Consolation Flowing Free

American Play-Party Song

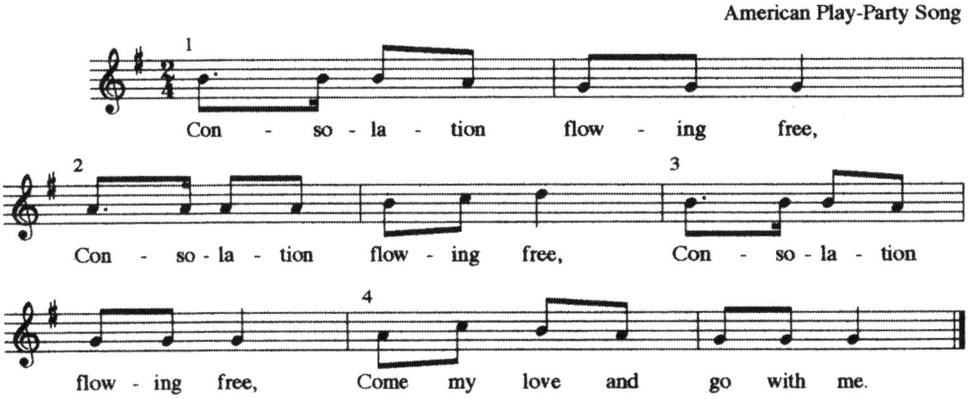

Description and Performance Suggestions:

Text: *Consolation* is yet another version of an ubiquitous folksong - *Go Tell Aunt Rhody* is perhaps its most familiar form - though it appears also in many variations, including an ode to second grade arithmetic, *Cancellation Flowing Free!* This one hails from the play-party era on the western frontier - it's a dance and a dialogue, a teasing, mocking invitation to "come and go with me". It alternates question-and-answer lines with verses about food, using the *Consolation* quatrain as an unstructured refrain.

Try reading it as a dance - to keep nimble feet moving. Then add characterizations: who is speaking which verse, and in what tone of voice? Keep your foot tapping - how long is the space between verses? Is that space constant or varied? Does verse 1 want to reappear? Where?

Tune: The tune appears in countless variants - two extremes being in hymnals (attributed to various composers) and in square dance versions for solo fiddle. One reason for its longevity must be its simplicity - it's almost simple-minded! Two paralled four measure phrases are almost identical rhythmically (a dotted figure in measure 3) and exactly identical harmonically - I I V I. The range is all of a fifth, the melodic curves gently contrasted. It takes about ten seconds to sing. Nursery rhyme stuff indeed - how in the name of music theory can we base an extended improvisation on this? Well, in the name of music theory (melodic, rhythmic and harmonic variation) you can't - but in the name of context, of characterization, you can.

Context: The context is, of course, a real dance. Therefore, set your foot tapping, and sing verse 1 in its light, invitational mocking tone. Then repeat it - ten seconds can't get a dance started. Sing all the verses, listening for possible text responses, and sensing how long you can stretch the "vamp" between verses. (In my thinking, the dance does not stop at these extensions: they are part of the basic structure.) Where is the loudest, rowdiest verse? the softest? What forms can you create with the use of verse 1 as a refrain? Is there one form that feels inevitably "right:"?

Interpretation:

Again, this is just one possible interpretation. With this rhythmic tune, the way the music looks on the page is far closer to the way it sounds to the ear than are our "chant" examples. So the "chant" variants of ornamentation, flexible tempo and punctuation pauses are inappropriate here. There are, however, enormous (and again un-notatable) variations that can be made in tone of voice, quality and quantity of accent, and speech inflections that play against the constant beat (and are thus forerunners of jazz).

Ornamentation and Variation:

As the verses continue, there should be constant play in the way the four-and-eight measure phrase is set within interludes of varying lengths. There can be metric change too; an added beat (in tempo) can provide time for a breath, or text inflection, which brings welcome variety to the regular pattern.

Irregular metric patterns (adding one or more beats, or one or more measures, or omitting the same) is great for singing, but wreaks havoc with traditional dance patterns. This device is often present in 'modern' dance.

Responses:

With the possible response that follows, again the answering voice is basically an echo, but within just heard text rhythms, rather than pitches. Melodic and canonic answers are apt to be difficult in tonal melodies, where the harmonic implications are stong - particularly when there are no long held notes. There's just no time to echo during the first hearing - but after that, any just heard phrase would work as an ostinato: "Consolation" or "flowing free" or "come my love". The one you choose is the one you hear now, today. The compositional fun is in creating an idea in this first response that itself becomes amplified and varied during the course of the piece.

In the example following, the answering voice is responding to a singing of the first verse which pictures a country dance setting, complete with oom-pah accompaniment. (The challenge is to suggest this in the single line singing, not literally to provide the accompaniment). The text always gives the ostinato rhythm for the following verse accompaniment. Here, "Come, my love" picks up, in its light syncopation, on the mocking quality of the just heard verse. And the same harmonic pattern is used for successive verses varied by text rhythms ("cannot go"; "Irish potatoes") rather than by more complex harmonies. (And if we should posit another answering voice, in a three-part setting, we can immediately engage in dialogue between the two answers - wit, invention, and humorous play that does not tamper with the integrity of the tune.) We are providing not melodic, harmonic and rhythmic variation of the tune itself, but play with form, characterization and setting, against which the tune appears both familiar and fresh for each verse.

mp
Con-so-la-tion flow-ing free, Con-so-la-tion flow-ing free, Con-so-la-tion
flow-ing free, Come my love and go with me.
p
Come, my love and go with
mf
Con-so-la-tion flow-ing free, Con-so-la-tion flow-ing free, Con-so-la-tion
mp
me. Con - so - la - tion, Con - so - la - tion,
flow-ing free, Come my love and go with me.
Verse 2. Con - so - la - tion, Come and go with me, Come and
(little girl's voices)
I'm too young, I can-not go, I'm too young, I can-not go, I'm too young I
(mocking)
go! can-not go, can-not go,
can-not go, can-not leave my Moth-er, O.
can-not go, can - not leave her, can - not leave her,
End of Verse 3.
(or)
leave your Moth-er, if you would. if you would.
leave her, if you would, if you would, to leave her,
Verse 4.
I-rish po-ta-toes, tops and all
etc.
to leave her if you would. I-rish po -
End of Verse 4.
Verse 5.
kiss her now or not at all. Ap-ples fried and
etc.
ta - toes kiss her now, kiss her now or not at all.

Buffalo Gals

American

2. As I was walkin' [down the street (*3x*)]
A purty gal I chanced to meet,
Oh, she was fair to view.
REFRAIN

3. I stopped her and we [had some talk, (*3x*)]
But her foot covered up the whole side-walk
And left no room for me
REFRAIN.

4. Purtiest gal I ever [seen in my life, (*3x*)]
Oh I wish to the Lord that she was my wife
And we would part no more.
REFRAIN

Hush, Little Baby

Appalachian Lullaby

2. If that mockingbird don't sing,

   Mama's goin' to buy you a wedding ring.

3. If that wedding ring turns brass,

   Mama's goin' to buy you a looking glass.

4. If that looking glass gets broke,

   Mama's goin' to buy you a billy goat.

5. If that billy goat runs away,

   Mama's goin' to buy you a horse and sleigh.

6. If that horse and sleigh turns over,

   Mama's goin' to buy you a dog named Rover.

7. If that dog named Rover won't bark

   Mama's goin' to buy you a pony cart.

8. If that pony cart runs away,

   Ta ra ra ra boom-de-ay.

In Balinderry

Irish

Jenny Jenkins

English Play-Party Song

2. O, will you wear red, O my dear, O my dear,
O, will you wear red, Jenny Jenkins?
I won't wear red, it's the color of my head,
I'll buy me a foldy roldy roll,
Jenny Jenkins, roll.

3. Green . . . It's a shame to be seen,

4. Blue . . . It's the color of a shoe,

5. Purple . . . It's the color of a turtle,

6. O, what will you wear, O my dear, O my dear,
O, what will you wear, Jenny Jenkins?
It's nothin' I'll wear, I'm - a gonna go bare!
I'll buy me a foldy roldy roll,
Jenny Jenkins roll.

Lowlands

American Sea Chanty

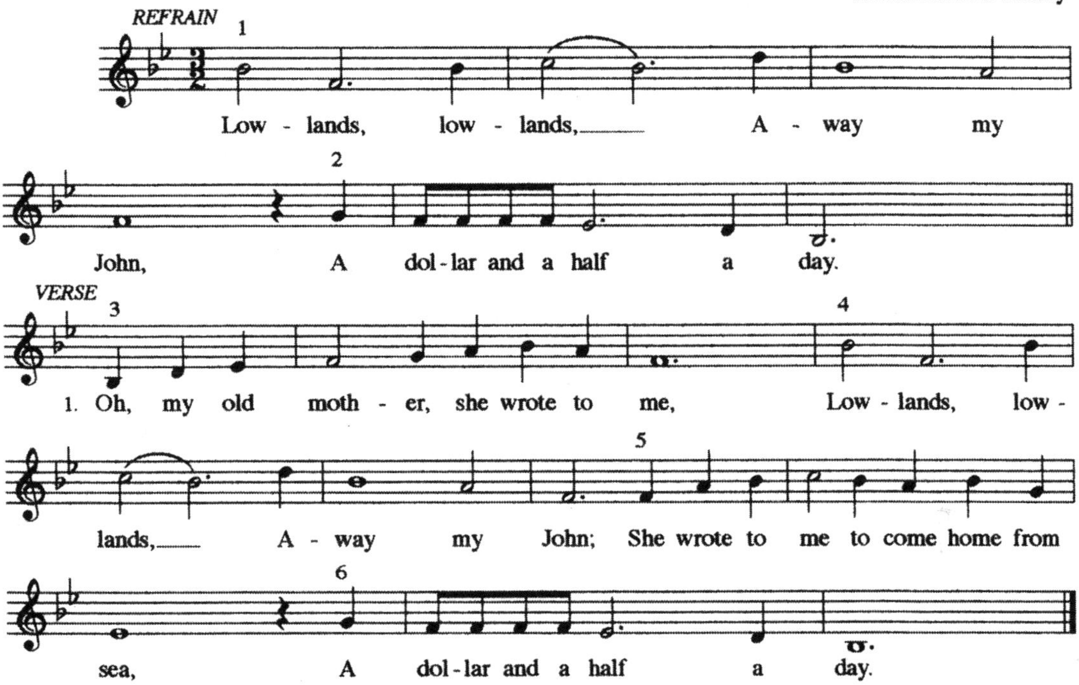

2. A dollar a day is a Hoosier's pay.
Lowlands, lowlands, away my John.
A dollar a day is a Hoosier's pay.
A dollar and a half a day.

3. All in the night my true love came.
Lowlands, lowlands, away my John.
All in the night my true love came.
A dollar and a half a day.

4. She came to me all in my sleep.
Lowlands, lowlands, away my John.
She came to me all in my sleep.
A dollar and a half a day.

5. And then I knew my love was dead.
Lowlands, lowlands, away my John.
And then I knew my love was dead.
A dollar and a half a day.

Polly Wolly Doodle

American Square Dance

2. Oh my Sal she was a maiden fair, Sing *etc.*

With curly eyes and laughing hair. Sing *etc.*

REFRAIN

3. Oh a grasshopper sat on a railroad track, Sing *etc.*

A-pickin' his teeth with a carpet tack. Sing *etc.*

REFRAIN

4. Oh I went to bed but it warn't no use, Sing *etc.*

'Cause my feet stuck out for a chicken roost. Sing *etc.*

REFRAIN

V. BLUES AND JAZZ MELODIES

These titles refer to music which arose from the transplanting of African peoples into the Americas. There is no doubt that they brought with them a host of vibrant artistic forms, and it is the collision of these traditions with those of European based 'white' music which changed the musical landscape then, and continues to do so now.

There are here unique qualities of both pitch and rhythm (microtones, slides, displacement of the beat, primacy of percussion, etc.) These elements derive from an aural/oral tradition which defies accurate notation: the ear simply hears differently from what the eye sees. There can be no exact parallel. There is also an infusion of improvisation into a very page-oriented traditon, which tends to take us back to the era before notation -- back to where this book started, with chant. Certainly 'free rhythm' creeps in at cadenzas and the wails found in solo, unaccompanied blues lines. Marches, rags and up-tempo hymns all contributed to the growth of super-rhythmic 'jazz', which is often instrumental rather than vocal. And there is a quantity of music which partakes of both styles. Imagine a slow, free introduction which moves into a lively and bouncy beat, often on the same melodic pattern. Indeed, it is even possible to have both at the same time: have you ever tried to notate the free, swinging solo of a brilliant saxophone player against the steady pulsing of the 'rhythm section'?

Blues, jazz and spirituals all spring from the same source, and are often difficult to separate. Spirituals have a sacred text (but can be jazzy or bluesy); Blues have a special timbre, a traditional (but often varied) 12 bar form; and Jazz is primarily (but not simply) rhythm, with intricate variations in both its melodic and time-measured elements. All are based originally on pared-down, singable melodies, which become infinitely varied over time and usage. The songs demand to be taken off the page: they cannot be sung as notated. Again, begin with language: find a 'southern' inflection, and explore the diphthongs, expressive consonants and dropped or elided syllables which characterize this idiom. 'Loaded' syllables must sound (even in the speaking) like their meaning. (Alexander Pope, in *An Essay on Criticism*, says "the sound must seem an echo to the sense".)

Coo Coo Bird

Appalachian Mountain Work Song

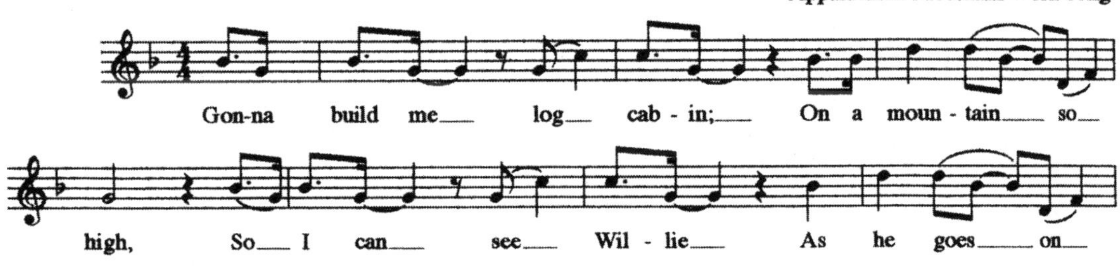

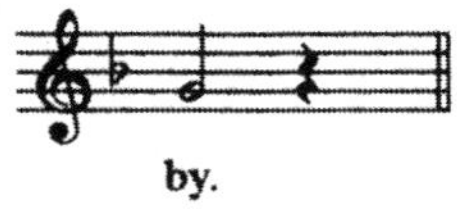

2. Oh, the coo coo is a pretty bird,
She wobbles as she flies.
She never hollers "coo coo"
Till the fourth day of July.

3. Jack of diamonds, jack of diamonds,
I've known you from old.
Now you robbed my poor pockets
Of my silver and gold.

Text: This minimal poem contains only two or three syllables in the short phrases, and five or six in the long. It is colloquial, southern, allusive, making use of familiar 'floating' lines in the 2nd and 3rd verses. The effect is breathless, as if sustained song were impossible. A raspy, blues voice is indicated.

Tune: Here is a play of short phrases separated by rests, by measured silences. It is a game of displaced accents, of syncopations, of a dialogue with an (unvoiced) steady, heavy beat. The natural minor scale is used, with a narrow range until the lower cadence points. The tessitura should be low, and husky.

Context: Is this possibly a work song? There is nothing in the text to indicate this, but everything in the beat suggests it, in what isn't voiced. How about a chain-gang, working on the railroad with heavy sledges: at each missing beat, the hammer descends with brute force, perhaps with a grunted "unh" from the singer. The text consists of random thought: home, the coo-coo bird, gambling.

Ornamentation and Variation: Think of a small jazz band, with a great cornet, or clarinet, or sax. How would they elaborate on the melody? Other 'blues' notes would creep in (non-scales tones are perfectly possible here), and more or less elaborate riffs. Try not only different instruments, but different responses to the successive verses.

Crawdad Song

Southern United States Game-dance

2. You get a line, I'll get a pole, honey;
You get a line, I'll get a pole, babe;
You get a line, I'll get a pole,
I'll meet you down at the crawdad hole,
Hon - ey, babe of mine.

3. Settin' on the ice, my feet got cold, honey;
Settin' on the ice, my feet got cold, babe;
Settin' on the ice, my feet got cold,
Watchin' that crawdad dig his hole,
Hon - ey, babe of mine.

4. Settin' on the bank, my feet got hot, honey;
Settin' on the bank, my feet got hot, babe;
Settin' on the ice, my feet got hot,
Watchin' that crawdad rack and trot,
Hon - ey, babe of mine.

This is truly an up-tempo song: it should go just as fast as you can speak the words. Get that southern accent in your voice: 'gal', 'moh-nin', 'bay-abe', 'Duh', 'yo'. Pretend that there is a drum set going lickey-split behind you, and you must fit the text to that unyielding beat. Pitches you *can* play with: try sliding into the first down-beat, and using two pitches (A-C) with a slide between on 'bay-abe' (think jazz clarinet). It's possible to ride right on the line between speech and song: vary the verses this way.

Text: An invitation -- but who is this'li'l gal'? A child? Or is this a courting song? Or a tease? The words quickly turn into nonsense, with the possiblity of innumerable improvised idiocies.

Tune: This pentatonic tune has long notes at the ends of phrases 1, 2 and 5, with the text squeezed into phrases 3 and 4. There are three repetitions of the first line, then one quick statement of the next, moving right into a refrain which changes from verse one to verse two. It's rather like winding up a spring toy which releases at phrase three...It's obviously a rhythm piece: if you were Sportin'Life, how would you move to this dance? How would you use your voice?

Responses: Those empty beats at the ends of phrases cry out for echoes, and there are wonderful word possibilities given: 'mornin', 'babe', 'so soon', 'honey', 'babe of mine'. One way of freeing your imagination here is to respond to a 'doo-bee-doo' textless singing of the tune (jazz clarinet) and pretend you are an answering clarinet, filling in the held notes with cascades of riffs. Then try the same thing with words only: can you find lots of ways to use the nonsense syllables to fill the beats? Last, try to get a text response that allows you the fun of the instrumental melodic answers. (Since it's a nonsense song, nonsense on the answers is perfectly in keeping).

Fare Thee Well

American Folk Blues

2. If I had wings like Noah's dove,
I'd fly up the river to the one I love,
Fare thee well, my honey, fare thee well.

3. Oh, one of these days and it won't be long,
You'll call my name, and I'll be gone,
Fare thee well, my honey, fare thee well.

Text: The poem is in a three-line form, with a repeated last line which seems to change focus in each verse. Again, the narrative is ambiguous, hinted at rather than clearly defined. Verse one gives us a personal definition of the 'blues'; the second invokes Noah's dove to carry the singer to his absent love; the third promises to hit the road, be gone, perhaps leave one 'honey' for another...or just to wander. The speech is very colloquial south: it shouldn't sound like the King's English.

Tune: This is a rhythm song: imagine a drum set with brushes holding a steady slow triplet beat in the background, against which the melody describes its lovely curves. Enjoy the octave jump to the high note in the 3rd phrase, and the long curve down to home. There is freedom in the relationships of the three lines: how long will you hold the final note in each one?

Context: This particular blues is not really sad, nor feeling an ultimate disillusion; there is a playful lilt, a teasing manner to it (now you see me, now you don't). Play with different southern accents as you sing; Virginia, Alabama and Texas should sound very different. Are you white or black? male or female? young or old? at home or in jail?...

One Possible Interpretation: Even in singing this tune as a solo without accompaniment, keep a pulse going securely in your inner ear. The quality of beat is supremely important here; the listener must sense that, like a good jazz player, you are taking all kinds of liberties over a very steady pulse.

Ornamentation and Variation: All I need to do is to think of different blues singers or instrumentalists to give me ideas of how to play with this tune. Begin with the simplicity of the pentatonic scale, then add 'blue' notes or other connecting pitches which ornament but do not destroy the original scale.

Responses: Try a literal echo of the end of each line while the melody holds: 'the blues ain't bad'; 'I ever had'; 'fare thee well'. Or the response can be very free, like a jazz clarinet response to a saxophone statement.

Ev'ry Night

American Folk Blues

2. I wish to the Lord the train would come, *(3x)*
And take me back where I come from.

3. 'Twas once my apron hung down low, *(3x)*
And now my apron's to my chin.

4. I wish to the Lord my babe was born, *(3x)*
A sitting on his Daddy's knee.

5. True love, don't weep, true love don't mourn, *(3x)*
I'm going back where I come from.

Green, Green, Rocky Road

Southern United States Game-Song

On repeated versus use other names. (Miss Suzy, Miss Bettie, Mr. Charley, etc.)

This Ol' Hammer

Black Work Song

2. Take this hammer to the Captain, *(3x)*

Tell him I'm gone,

Tell him I'm gone.

3. If he asks you what's the matter, *(3x)*

Tell him you don't know,

Tell him you don't know.

4. If he asks you was I running, *(3x)*

Tell him no!

Tell him no!

Tip Around My Bed

American Spiritual

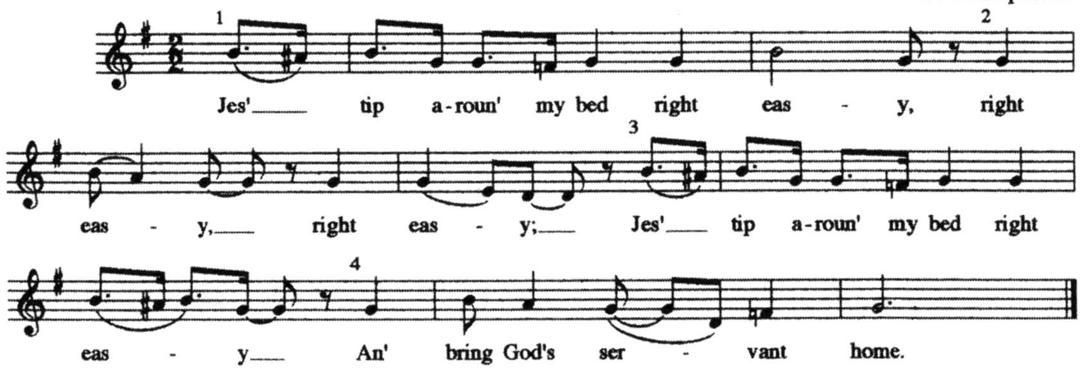

2. Just low down the chariot [right easy. (3x)]
And bring God's servant home.

3. Just turn my bed around [right easy. (3x)]
And bring God's servant home.

4. Just turn my cover back [right easy. (3x)]
And bring God's servant home.

5. Oh, low down, death, [right easy. (3x)]
And bring God's servant home.

Trav'lin' Shoes

American Spiritual

VI. NOTES ON THE SONGS

Chapter I

Black, Black, Black ABBA'

One of the oldest melodies in the book, this is a modal tune which seems to be in d-to-d 'dorian', until the final unexpected "E". Allow this to be the last note -- don't resolve it to D, or harmonize it with an A major chord. It will tip you into the next verse each time, and, at the end, make it feel as if the song were unending -- this love affair is indeed unresolved...
Note the ABBA' form, with the subtle variation of the last line. Sing the word-rhythms: where can you lengthen? pause? hurry? vary? Draw the mood-scheme of the verses. Where is the climax? What is the mood at the end?

By'm Bye AA B C D (AA) D (A)

This simple going-to-bed song seems so artless as to be completely improvised. But it is wonderfully constructed on its five-note scale, with subtle repetitions and a lovely octave jump in the D phrase, repeated at the end. How freely can you speak it? sing it? *By'm Bye* are words made for an ostinato: on what pitches (drawn from the melody) can you sing them? How do you vary the verses when only the numbers change?

He's Gone Away ABAB'AC

This is often performed with a steady beat, so if you know it this way, try to wean yourself away from it. Try leaving long and unmeasured spaces between the lines of the poem. Hold the words 'stay', 'comin', 'goes' and of course 'miles'. Then the verse may move more quickly -- but don't be rigid with the beat. Which are the important syllables? How can you stress them, and make them different from one another? Enjoy the 'ps' of 'lips'...
In songs with a refrain, make sure it is varied on each repetition, probably growing more complex each time, with the verses staying simple to allow the text to be heard. In the responses, try echoing, and even a canon on the refrain. The coda should echo and fade away into nothing.

Chapter II

Buckeye Jim ABCC'D

Feel the comfortable rocking-chair motion of this song, and sing as if to a small child. This is American vernacular speech: try 'you *cain't* go', and enjoy the rhythm of 'buckeye' (which is a kind of horse chestnut tree; Ohio is the Buckeye State). There are only two lines of verse (so it's easy to improvise more), followed by three short varied phrases of refrain. Does it want to stop at the end? How much echo can it take? How do you get the baby to sleep?

How Can I Keep From Singing ABAB'CC'DB

A soaring melody, of beautifully shaped phrase curves, this is a song that celebrates vocal richness in both words and music. Keep the stately three-beat rhythm throughout, but play gently with the eighth notes at "all the tumult" to reflect the words' rhythms and meaning. Notice the accumulation of tension in the 'C' phrases (ending at the high point), and then the consolation of 'D' in each verse (ending at the low point), leading to the final poignant question.
Make a plan of dynamics for the whole text, to guide your progression. With the answering voice, try imitation at different times: where does it work? Using only the notes in the melody, decide which tone belongs at the end of each phrase; when do you want to sound 'at home'? 'away'? How do you sustain tension? resolve it?

The Riddle Song ABBA'

Another early English melody with many variants, this pentatonic tune is also modal, with its "C" ending. Again, don't try to change it, or harmonize it with F major: it is not tonal! This could be a love song, or a children's game, or a lullaby; how do you find it most evocative? Take time to ask the simple question in each line with a change of vocal color. In the responses, try echoes and canons, even pedals. Make sure the text is clear in verse 3; 'pippin' is the chick just before it's hatched. Can you depict a sleeping baby at the end?

Chapter III

I Know Where I'm Goin' ABCD

One of the loveliest of old ballads, this is the musing of a privileged young lady, thinking about her love for a scalawa, perhaps a gypsy or sailor ('black' doesn't refer to *race* but rather *outside the conventions*) who is forbidden to her. (I always think of Juliet and Romeo.) The loose form makes it feel improvised; the scale seems firmly tonic with the ascending triad outlined in each of the first three phrases. But then comes the wonderful final curve, with its ambiguous ending on A...Sing it with a different tonal quality -- perhaps a question, or a 'lonesome' sound on the first and last verses. To whom are you singing? How do they respond?

Soldier, Soldier A B C D

This is a lovely dorian melody, with a beautiful curve, a rhythm which both affirms and denies a basic march-beat, and several refrains. 'For O the fife and drum' is one possible ostinato; so are 'Soldier, soldier', 'How can I marry such a pretty girl as you?' and 'Now soldier, put them on'. And the even numbered verses serve as refrains to the odd ones. Probably the least imaginative way to sing this song is to alternate women and men according to the text. Rather, it is a ballad, a story, which should be told in one voice with imaginative coloring. It's also a children's game song; it can be a lullaby (except for the last line, which can by sung with infinite regret). Of course there are many more verses. If you sing it as a ballad accompanying yourself on the guitar, you learn to make each verse varied in color, phrasing and rhythm. In a choral setting, keep as much of that solo quality as possible, and make the accompanying voices proved the steady rhythm and harmonic background of the guitar. In this case, also hunt for little imitations, brief canons.

The Chickens They Are Crowing A B A' C

I love the modal quality of this tune; it's a true mixolydian, and never seems to come to rest. Read the text as a story: who is singing? man or woman? young or old? What is the mood? cocky? confident? questioning? doubtful? There are only two lines in each verse, with built-in repetition: what openings are there for responses? If you could choose an instrument for accompaniment, what would it be? Why? Does that give you an idea for the responding voice?

Weevily Wheat A B C D A B C D

Here is another mixolydian tune, very diferent in mood. Enjoy the recurrring F-natural, both high and low. Think a rowdy kind of square dance, with a toe-tapping beat and strong first-beat accents. The first note is a 'gathering' note: it can be held until everyone is paying attention (but only on the first verse). It's also a love-song from the woman's point of view, but with a very hard-headed and humorous asssesment of that charming scoundrel, Charley. (Look up some of the missing verses.) Take a cue from the frontier grammar; 'I don't want none', 'He can do it handy', and sing in a back-country tone of voice. The word 'Charley' makes a fine ostinato: try improvising different phrases within the mode on just this one word. This song goes at such a pace that the only time for an answer is at the conclusion of the refrain: how many measures can you interpolate? the same number each time, or should it vary? Where is the climax? How can you stop all this energy?

What Shall We Do With the Drunken Sailor A B A' C A B A' C

This is a dorian tune, packed full of energy. It cries out for unaccompained men's voices, full of teasing bravado. Get the fast beat established, and don't lose it. The underlying harmonies are given in the tune: don't add more chord changes, or you'll slow it up. (What chords make the cadence?) Use the refrains to build sonorities: the slower-moving text allows more vocalization, and imitation becomes more possible. Play with time; set each verse up with an introduction, and be prepared for a long coda!

Chapter IV

Buffalo Gals AA' BB'

This is a play-party song, acted out by young people who were forbidden to dance, but who figured out that they could 'move to the music'. I like a moderate tempo with a light beat, like a 'soft-shoe' dance. Keep the tone of invitation, of flirtation, of back-woods tall-tale spinning and then sentimentality. Find the basic harmonic structure, and neither change it nor improve on it: accept it, and make your choral setting through reponses to the text and imaginative ways of voicing those chords. (Think guitar and stand-up bass).

Hush Li'l Baby A B

Only two lines long, this is the shortest song in the book. It is exactly right as a lullaby, sung with gentle humor and a steady, rocking beat. How can you set up the beat? continue it? vary it? Is the melody always in the same voice? Can you add measures between verses? What are possible responding texts? How busy should the setting be?

In Balinderry A A' B C

I found this in a collection of Irish tunes, and it immediately lodged in my memory as one of the sweetest songs of remembered love. There are only the two verses, simple yet implying so much. Could it be a spinning song? What is the underlying rhythm? How strong is the harmonic compulsion? Would it be possible to do with a drone (i.e. bagpipes)?

Jenny Jenkins A A'B C D

There are almost as many versions of this tune as there are singers: one rarely sees the same nonsense syllables in the next-to-last phrase. It's also the kind of song where the poetic imagination and bravado of the singer is the only limit to the number of verses. In this case, the boy-girl dialogue seems just right for those lines, with a wonderful mix-up on the refrain. Can you play with the refrain: lengthen it? imitate note? vary the meter? the notes? How do you set the last verse? Think dance all the way through, or at least see the protagonists in your mind's eye, and get their body language in to the setting.

Lowlands A B C A D B

It's a sea chanty, but a fo' castle song, not a work song. Sung at a slow tempo, it has a mesmerizing quality, totally at odds with the text. ('A dollar and a half a day' is a 'floating verse' found in many work songs.) Sung richly, it generates tone, building up waves of reverberation which are full of nostalgia, of regret, of a waking dream. Find the wonderfully vocal legato tone inherent in the melody, and then let echoes accumulate around it. 'Lowlands' make a wonderful ostinato.

Polly Wolly Doodle A B A' B' C B A 'B'

This bit of tom-foolery is pure Americana, reminiscent of the minstrel show. The nonsensical text continually stretches for ridiculous rhymes, while the monotonous tune breaks out of a middle register only in the 'B' phrase, and out of bubbling eight-note rhythms at the beginning of the refrain. Since it is so completely playful, the arranger can have carte blanche to use all the tricks of the trade. Play games with the singers and listeners: avoid the expected. Just don't overload the poor song and sink it!

Chapter V

Ev'ry Night A A' A" B

This is an amalgam of classic 3-line blues and the much more traditional 4-line folk stanza, with three statements of line 1. In both cases, tension is built up to be resolved in the final line. The melody here has a classic curve reaching its height in the third phrase and coming to rest in the last. The text is a collection of fairly standard folk verse: the train is particulary helpful here as an image for rhythmic development. (There are many verses in different versions: hunt them out.) This tune is particularly blues-derived in that it demands the most complex harmonic treatment of all the songs in this collection. Try making a simple chord outline, and then flesh it out with more motion, using 7ths, 9ths, 11ths and passing dissonances. Imagine a creamy clarinet solo on the melody, add the drumset with a slow back-beat, and then listen to those five and six beat holes between phrases. Which instrument is responding? how? Now can you translate that sound to voices? Who is answering? with what text?

Green, Green, Rocky Road A A' A" A"' (x) B B B' C

A delightful children's game song from Alabama, this has elements of old English folk rhyme mixed with a very jazzy beat and the kind of 'choosing' game played by young and old all over the world. Two notable features here are the opening pitches that put us into a bluesy world, and the unchanging refrain 'rocky road'. I can see a jump-rope group, with the jumper gasping out the lines and the whole group of little kids chanting the response. Another picture would be the play-party, with the calling out of the name most likely to be embarrassing, and that person having to endure the public kissing as well as being 'it' for the next round. The music changes radically from the first half to the second: keep them distinct, and always enjoy going back to the refrain. Where does the song end? How?

This Ol' Hammer A A' A B

As in most black music, this song implies enormous rhythmic energy. There's no way it can be sung like 'Consolation Flowing Free': there's an enormously physical response to the beat. Set your tempo first: think of the men with sledge-hammers laying railroad track -- that's the tone quality. For the responses, think another worker facing you across the track, echoing your phrases. What happens on the last phrase? How is one verse different from another?

Tip Around My Bed A B A C

Perhaps the best way to become acquainted with this song is to ignore the words, and hear the melody as a jazz tune in a kind of 'medium swing' beat. Can you begin to hear the 'bent' pitches? the variants of syncopation? It's written here in mixolydian mode: it's of course possible to hear it as major, or, best of all, half-way between the two. Can you sing in the crack between F natural and F sharp? When you've got the beat and the swing going, add the text. Picture the singer (old?), on his or her death bed, inviting a welcome Death to come closer, and 'bring God's servant home'. What depth of faith -- and of tender humor -- does it take to invoke Death in this way? (Is 'tip' short for 'tip-toe'?) How can you color the verse differently? Where is the climax, or maximum sonority? How does it end? For responses, you can't get much better than 'right easy', or the repeated last line.

Trav'lin' Shoes A B C D A' B' C D

Think of these 'Trav'lin Shoes' as being tap shoes, and the dancer as seductively evil as Sportin' Life in *Porgy and Bess*. This devil will tempt all but the most determined to follow him: the song just hints at the titanic struggle between the sinner, determined to live, and Death, equally strong, determined to win. Can you see the dance-duet between them? Feel the rhythm in your bones. Dance before you sing, then let the song glide along the top of the beats. We have here only one verse to work with: how long can you keep it going? It's possible to research or make-up new verses, but I love the challenge of just having one, and the freedom it gives you to become more and more adventurous in the ways you transform the melody. *Responses*: look at all the echo possibilties, as well as ostinati like "Come an'go" or "trav'lin' shoes". There's nothing dour or fatalistic about this song: don't let either contestant win!